HOW TO PASS THE CMA EXAM:
A SYSTEM FOR SUCCESS

TABLE OF CONTENTS

This booklet's purpose is to help you develop and implement a **SYSTEM FOR SUCCESS** for passing the CMA exam, which includes

1. **Understanding the CMA exam process, including the purpose of the exam, subject matter coverage, preparation, format, administration, grading, and pass rates**

2. **Learning and understanding the subject matter tested**

3. **Perfecting your question-answering techniques by answering questions under exam conditions**

4. **Planning and practicing exam execution**

5. **Developing the confidence you need to succeed**

Each of these five steps is discussed and illustrated on the following pages. Gleim removes the "mystique" of the CMA exam by providing you with the answers, information, and tools you need to arrive at the test center with a head start, **plus** the confidence necessary to PASS.

"EXAM SUCCESS GUARANTEED!"

The Gleim CMA Review System GUARANTEES that you will pass each part on the first try. The system combines our books, CMA Test Prep, Audio Review, Gleim Online, Essay Wizard, Exam Rehearsal™, and access to a Personal Counselor to maximize your available study time. Because we identify and focus on your weak areas, you will not spend any more time preparing than is necessary to guarantee success.

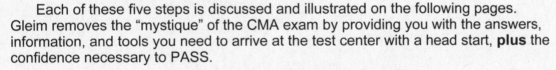

Gleim Publications, Inc.
P.O. Box 12848
University Station
Gainesville, Florida 32604
(888) 87-GLEIM or (888) 874-5346
(352) 375-0772
Fax: (352) 375-6940
Internet: www.gleim.com
Email: admin@gleim.com

For updates to this edition of *How to Pass the CMA Exam: A System for Success*

Go To: www.gleim.com/CMAupdate

Or: Email update@gleim.com with **CMA SFS 2015-1** in the subject line. You will receive our current update as a reply.

Updates are available until the next edition is published.

ISBN: 978-1-58194-491-4 *CMA Review: Part 1*
ISBN: 978-1-58194-492-1 *CMA Review: Part 2*
ISBN: 978-1-58194-508-9 *CMA System for Success*

First Printing: August 2014

ACKNOWLEDGMENTS

The authors are indebted to the Institute of Certified Management Accountants (ICMA) for permission to use problem materials from past CMA examinations and other ICMA exam information. Questions and unofficial answers from the Certified Management Accountant Examinations, copyright © 1982 through 2014 by the Institute of Certified Management Accountants, are reprinted and/or adapted with permission.

Environmental Statement -- This book is printed on high-quality, environmentally friendly groundwood paper, sourced from certified sustainable forests and produced either TCF (totally chlorine-free) or ECF (elementally chlorine-free). Our recyclable paper is more porous than coated paper, so we recommend marking it with a non-bleed-through highlighter.

This publication is designed to provide accurate and authoritative information with regard to the subject matter covered. It is sold with the understanding that the publisher is not engaged in rendering legal, accounting, or other professional service.

If legal advice or other expert assistance is required, the services of a competent professional person should be sought.

(From a declaration of principles jointly adopted by a Committee of the American Bar Association and a Committee of Publishers.)

AUTHOR

Irvin N. Gleim is a Professor Emeritus in the Fisher School of Accounting at the University of Florida and is a member of the American Accounting Association, Academy of Legal Studies in Business, American Institute of Certified Public Accountants, Association of Government Accountants, Florida Institute of Certified Public Accountants, The Institute of Internal Auditors, and the Institute of Management Accountants. He has had articles published in the *Journal of Accountancy*, *The Accounting Review*, and *The American Business Law Journal* and is author/coauthor of numerous accounting and aviation books and CPE courses.

REVIEWERS AND CONTRIBUTORS

Garrett Gleim, B.S., CPA (not in public practice), is a graduate of the Wharton School at the University of Pennsylvania. Mr. Gleim coordinated the production staff, reviewed the manuscript, and provided production assistance throughout the project.

Grady M. Irwin, J.D., is a graduate of the University of Florida College of Law, and he has taught in the University of Florida College of Business. Mr. Irwin provided substantial editorial assistance throughout the project.

Michael Kustanovich, M.A., CPA, is a graduate of Ben-Gurion University of the Negev in Israel. He is a Lecturer of Accountancy in the Department of Accountancy at the University of Illinois at Urbana-Champaign. He has worked in the audit departments of KPMG and PWC and as a financial accounting lecturer in the Department of Economics of Ben-Gurion University of the Negev. Mr. Kustanovich provided substantial editorial assistance throughout the project.

Lawrence Lipp, J.D., CPA (Registered), is a graduate from the Levin College of Law and the Fisher School of Accounting at the University of Florida. Mr. Lipp provided substantial editorial assistance throughout the project.

A PERSONAL THANKS

This manual would not have been possible without the extraordinary effort and dedication of Jacob Brunny, Julie Cutlip, Eileen Nickl, Tiffany Schwan, Teresa Soard, Justin Stephenson, Joanne Strong, Elmer Tucker, and Candace Van Doren, who typed the entire manuscript and all revisions and drafted and laid out the diagrams and illustrations in this book.

The authors appreciate the production and editorial assistance of Jessica Felkins, Jim Harvin, Chris Hawley, Jeanette Kerstein, Katie Larson, Diana León, Cary Marcous, Shane Rapp, Drew Sheppard, and Martha Willis.

The authors also appreciate the critical reading assistance of Jared Armenti, Jeff Bennett, Coryn Brewer, Ellen Buhl, Paul Davis, Mikaila Gazzillo, Jack Hahne, Bethany Harris, Melissa Leonard, Yating Li, Jerry Mathis, Monica Metz, Daniel Sinclair, Tingwei Su, Nanan Toure, Dustin Wallace, Diana Weng, Kenneth Wilbur, and Hailun Zhu.

Finally, we appreciate the encouragement, support, and tolerance of our families throughout this project.

STUDY UNIT ONE
THE CMA EXAMINATION: AN OVERVIEW AND PREPARATION INTRODUCTION

(10 pages of outline)

CMA Exam

Part	1	2
Formal Title	Financial Reporting, Planning, Performance, and Control	Financial Decision Making
Exam Length	4 hours	4 hours
No. of Questions		
Multiple-Choice	100	100
Essay	2	2

This study unit will give you an overview of the ICMA's CMA exam and our suggested method of preparation.

CMA is the acronym for Certified Management Accountant. The CMA exam is developed and offered by the Institute of Certified Management Accountants (ICMA) in numerous domestic and international locations.

1.1 FOLLOW THESE STEPS TO PASS THE EXAM

1. Read the **Introduction** of your Gleim CMA Review book to familiarize yourself with the content and structure of each part of the CMA exam. In the Introduction, you will find

    a. An **overview of each part** and what it generally tests, including the ICMA's Content Specification Outlines (CSOs)

    b. Details on how to **organize your study schedule** to make the most out of each resource in the Gleim CMA Review System (i.e., books, CMA Test Prep, Audio Review, Gleim Online, Essay Wizard, Exam Rehearsals, etc.)

    c. Tactics for your **actual test day**, including

        1) Time budgeting, so you complete all questions with time to review
        2) Question-answering techniques to obtain every point you can
        3) An explanation of how to be in control of your CMA exam

2. Scan this Gleim *How to Pass the CMA Exam: A System for Success* booklet and note where to revisit later in your studying process to obtain a deeper understanding of the CMA exam.

    a. *How to Pass the CMA Exam: A System for Success* has seven study units:

        Study Unit 1: The CMA Examination: An Overview and Preparation Introduction
        Study Unit 2: ICMA Content Specification Outlines
        Study Unit 3: Content Preparation, Test Administration, and Performance Grading
        Study Unit 4: Multiple-Choice Questions
        Study Unit 5: Essay Questions
        Study Unit 6: Preparing to Pass the CMA Exam
        Study Unit 7: How to Take the CMA Exam

3. BEFORE you begin studying, you may wish to take a **Diagnostic Quiz** at www.gleim.com/QuizCMA.

    a. The Diagnostic Quiz includes a representative sample of 40 multiple-choice questions and can help determine which part of the exam you want to take first and/or how much time you need to devote to studying particular topic areas.

    b. When you are finished, you can access a Review Session and consult with a **Personal Counselor** to better focus your review on any areas in which you have less confidence.

4. Follow the steps outlined in Study Unit 6, Subunit 5, "How to Use the Gleim Review System." This is the **study plan** that our most successful candidates adhere to. Study until you have reached your **desired proficiency level** (e.g., 75%) for each study unit.

    a. As you proceed, be sure to check any **Updates** that may have been released.

        1) Gleim Online, Essay Wizard, CMA Test Prep, and Exam Rehearsals are updated automatically.
        2) Book updates can be viewed at www.gleim.com/CMAupdate, or you can have them emailed to you. See the information box in the top right corner of page ii for details.

    b. **Review this *How to Pass the CMA Exam: A System for Success* booklet** and become completely comfortable with what will be expected from you on test day.

5. Shortly before your test date, take an **Exam Rehearsal** (complimentary with the purchase of the Gleim CMA Review System!) at www.gleim.com/RehearseCMA.

    a. This timed and scored exam emulates the actual CMA exam and tests you not only on the content you have studied, but also on the question-answering and time-management techniques you have learned throughout the Gleim study process.

    b. When you have completed the exam, study your results to discover where you should **focus your review during the final days before your exam**.

6. **Take and PASS** your selected part of the CMA exam!

    a. When you have completed the exam, please contact Gleim at www.gleim.com/feedbackCMA with your **suggestions, comments, and corrections**. We want to know how well we prepared you for your testing experience.

1.2 EXAM FORMAT

The total exam is 8 hours of testing. It is divided into two parts, as follows:

Part 1 – Financial Reporting, Planning, Performance, and Control
Part 2 – Financial Decision Making

Each part consists of 100 multiple-choice questions and 2 essay scenarios, and testing lasts 4 hours (3 hours for the multiple-choice questions plus 1 hour for the essays). The exams are only offered during the following three testing windows: January/February, May/June, and September/October.

1.3 PURPOSE OF THE EXAMINATION

According to the IMA, the "CMA is the advanced professional certification specifically designed to measure the accounting and financial management skills that drive business performance."

In their Resource Guide, the ICMA explains that through the certification test, "the requirements of the CMA Program . . . recognize those who can demonstrate that they possess a sufficient degree of knowledge and skills in the areas of management accounting and financial management. In this way, the ICMA helps identify practitioners who have met certain predetermined professional standards."

1.4 THE INSTITUTE OF MANAGEMENT ACCOUNTANTS (IMA)

Conceived as an educational organization to develop the individual management accountant professionally and to provide business management with the most advanced techniques and procedures, the IMA was founded as the National Association of Cost Accountants in 1919 with 37 charter members. It grew rapidly, with 2,000 applications for membership in the first year, and today it is the largest management accounting association in the world, with members and chapters in the U.S. and abroad.

Membership in the IMA is open to all persons interested in advancing their knowledge of accounting or financial management. It is required for CMA candidates and CMAs. There are four types of membership: Regular, Student, Young Professional, and Academic. Fees for IMA members include a one-time membership application fee (for all new members except Students and Young Professionals) and an annual membership renewal fee. Members who have passed the CMA exam will also need to pay an annual maintenance fee, due at the same time as the renewal fee.

Go to www.gleim.com/CMAfees for the most current IMA membership fees.

Apply for IMA membership online at www.imanet.org/ima_membership.aspx.

1.5 THE INSTITUTE OF CERTIFIED MANAGEMENT ACCOUNTANTS (ICMA)

The only function of the ICMA is to offer and administer the CMA designation. This office is where exam content is reviewed to ensure it is up-to-date and relevant, new exam questions are prepared, and all records are kept.

The ICMA Board of Regents is a special committee of the IMA established to direct the CMA program for management accountants through the ICMA. Along with the ICMA staff, the Board undertakes all of the day-to-day work with respect to the CMA program.

1.6 SUBJECT MATTER TESTED

The ICMA has developed Content Specification Outlines (CSOs) and has committed to follow them on each examination. In addition to the CSOs, the ICMA has published Learning Outcome Statements (LOSs) that specify what you should be able to do.

Candidates for the CMA designation are expected to have a minimum level of business knowledge that transcends all examination parts. This minimum level includes knowledge of basic financial statements, time value of money concepts, and elementary statistics. Specific discussion of the ICMA's Levels of Performance (A, B, and C) is provided in Study Unit 2.

We continually adjust the content of our materials to reflect any changes in the ICMA's CSOs and LOSs. The CSOs for each part are presented in Study Unit 2, Subunits 2 and 3, beginning on page 13. The complete outlines are presented along with cross-references to the relevant Gleim study units/subunits for each topic.

The listing below contains the main sections for each part of the exam. The percentage coverage of each topic is indicated to its right.

Authors' note: CMA Review covers all of the CSO topics as they are tested on the CMA exam. When you take the exam, there will be no surprises.

ICMA'S CMA CONTENT SPECIFICATION OUTLINE OVERVIEW				
Part 1: Financial Reporting, Planning, Performance, and Control			**Part 2: Financial Decision Making**	
			Financial Statement Analysis	25%
External Financial Reporting Decisions	15%		Corporate Finance	20%
Planning, Budgeting, and Forecasting	30%		Decision Analysis	20%
Performance Management	20%		Risk Management	10%
Cost Management	20%		Investment Decisions	15%
Internal Controls	15%		Professional Ethics	10%

We have divided the overall task of preparing for the CMA exam into an appropriate number of study units for each part of the exam. As you will see in the Study Unit 2 cross-references, these study units cover all of the topics in the ICMA's CSOs.

1.7 WHEN TO APPLY AND TAKE THE EXAM

The CMA exam is offered during three testing windows each year: January/February, May/June, and September/October. Candidates may only sit for the exams during these windows.

Register about 6 weeks before the time you wish to take the exam. Registration for Parts 1 and 2 received on or after February 16, June 16, or October 16 will be authorized for any future testing window (i.e., not the current window, but the next window or later). For example, if you register for a part on February 16, 2015, the earliest you can take the exam is May 1, 2015. Registrations received before those dates will be authorized for any window including the current one. See the table on the following page.

If you register during	The earliest you can take your exam is
October 16-February 15	January/February
February 16-June 15	May/June
June 16-October 15	September/October

1.8 EXAM ADMINISTRATION

Examinations are administered by computer at hundreds of Prometric testing centers across the United States and internationally. Test centers are located in most metropolitan areas. For help locating Prometric test centers that offer the CMA exam, visit www.prometric.com/ICMA and click "Locate a Test Center."

1.9 EXAM FEES

Effective July 1, 2014

	Entrance Fee	Exam Fee One Part/Window	Rescheduling/ Cancelation Fee*
Regular	$240	$395	$50
Student	$75	$296.25	$50
Academic	$75	$197.50	$50

*This fee is applicable to candidates who reschedule/cancel their exam within 30 days of their appointment. Prior to 30 days, there is no penalty.

1.10 STEPS TO BECOME A CMA

1. Become knowledgeable about the exam, and determine which part you will take first.

2. Purchase the Gleim CMA Review System (including books, CMA Test Prep, Audio Review, Gleim Online, Essay Wizard, Exam Rehearsal, and access to a Personal Counselor) to thoroughly prepare for the CMA exam. Commit to systematic preparation for the exam as described in our review materials, including this booklet.

3. Set up your Study Planner in Gleim Online to design a personalized study schedule that meets your needs. Then, communicate with your Personal Counselor to ensure you are studying effectively. Call (888) 874-5346, ext. 498, or email PersonalCounselor@gleim.com.

4. Apply for membership in the IMA and enter the ICMA's certification program (Subunit 1.11 has details on the necessary steps).

5. Register online to take the desired part of the exam. Subunit 1.7 has more information on when each part of the exam is offered. You will receive authorization to take the exam from the ICMA and will need to sit for the exam in the appropriate testing window based on when you registered as designated by the ICMA (Subunit 1.13, "How to (1) Apply for, (2) Register for, and (3) Schedule Your CMA Exam").

6. Schedule your test with Prometric (online, national 800 number, or call your local Prometric testing site).

7. Work systematically through each study unit in the Gleim CMA Review System.

8. Sit for and PASS the CMA exam while you are in control, as described in Study Unit 7 of this booklet. Gleim Guarantees Success!

9. Email or call Gleim or visit www.gleim.com/feedbackCMA with your comments on our study materials and how well they prepared you for the exam.

10. Enjoy your career, pursue multiple certifications (CIA, CPA, EA, etc.), and recommend Gleim to others who are also taking these exams. Stay up-to-date on your Continuing Professional Education requirements with Gleim CPE.

1.11 THE ICMA'S REQUIREMENTS FOR CMA DESIGNATIONS

The CMA designation is granted only by the ICMA. Candidates must complete the following steps to become a CMA:

1. Become a **member** of the IMA and pay the Certification Entrance Fee.
2. Register for and schedule to take the desired part of the exam.
3. Pass both parts of the **exam** within **3 years**.
4. Satisfy the education requirement.
5. Satisfy the experience requirement.
6. **Comply** with the IMA's *Statement of Ethical Professional Practice*.

1.12 EDUCATION AND EXPERIENCE REQUIREMENTS

Education. Candidates seeking admission to the CMA program must hold a bachelor's degree, in any area, from an accredited college or university. A listing of domestic and international institutions that will be accepted by the ICMA without any evaluation can be found at http://univ.cc/world.php. Degrees from nonaccredited institutions must be evaluated by an independent agency listed at www.aice-eval.org or www.naces.org.

NOTE: Educational credentials must be submitted when applying or within 7 years of passing the examination. The educational credentials must qualify in order to be certified.

Experience. Two continuous years of **professional experience** in financial management and/or management accounting are required any time prior to or within 7 years of passing the examination.

- To qualify, employment must be in a position that requires regular involvement in the principles of management accounting and financial management, e.g., financial analysis, budget preparation, management information systems analysis, etc. See the ICMA's CMA Handbook for a complete list of qualifying positions, guidelines for part-time positions, and some examples of non-qualifying positions.

1.13 HOW TO (1) APPLY FOR, (2) REGISTER FOR, AND (3) SCHEDULE YOUR CMA EXAM

The information below summarizes the steps to become a member of the IMA, apply to the CMA certification program, and register to take an exam part at Prometric. You should read through these steps so you are completely comfortable when you begin the process for yourself. Detailed instructions and screenshots for every step of the application and registration program can be found at www.gleim.com/accounting/cma/steps. You can track your progress and organize your documentation with the help of our CMA Exam Worksheet at the end of this booklet.

STEP
1. Apply for Membership to the IMA
2. Enroll in the Certification Program
3. Register for One or More Parts of the Exam
4. Schedule Your Exam at Prometric

1. Apply for membership to the IMA.

   a. Go to the IMA's website (www.imanet.org) and click on the "IMA Membership" tab. Then, select your country of residence.

   b. Choose the type of membership you would like to purchase, and click the relevant "Join Today" link.

    c.   You now need to log in. If you are a new user of the IMA's website and have no current log-in information, you must create an account by clicking the "Click here to register" link, fill out the required information, and click "Register." Then you will need to navigate back to the membership application by clicking "Membership Products" in the navigation menu on the left. Now repeat Step b. on the previous page.

    d.   Now, you must select the chapter you will join upon becoming a member. Then, click "Continue."

    e.   You will be directed to your shopping cart. Note that there is an alert that reads "Information Needed." Click this alert.

        1)   You must now read and agree to abide by the IMA's *Statement of Ethical Professional Practice*. Once you have read the text, check the box and then click "Next." You may be asked to enter other relevant information based on the type of membership you are applying for (i.e., educational information for a Student Membership, etc.). When all relevant questions have been answered, you will see that the alert now reads "Ready for Checkout." Click "Checkout" to continue.

    f.   You will now need to fill out your payment information and click "Process My Order."

    g.   You will be taken to an "Order Summary" page with your order number and all relevant order information. You should print this page for your records. In addition, you will immediately receive a payment confirmation email and a "Welcome to the IMA" email. Your "Welcome to the IMA" email will contain your Member ID. You should read and save both emails.

2.   Enroll in the CMA certification program.

    a.   Go to the IMA's website (www.imanet.org), click on "Login" at the top of the page and fill in the username (Member ID) and password provided in the "Welcome to IMA" email you received.

    b.   Now, click on "Online Store" on the right-hand side of the page.

    c.   Click "Become a CMA" in the top row.

    d.   Click the "Add to Cart" box for the correct CMA Entrance Fee.

NOTE: Be sure to complete this step before you register to take a part of the exam.

    e.   Once your screen shows confirmation that the Entrance Fee has been added to your shopping cart, click the "Certification" link in the navigation menu on the left.

3.   Register to take the desired part(s) of the exam.

    a.   Do **not** register to take a part of the exam until you have successfully enrolled in the CMA certification program. If you fail to purchase entrance into the program, the system will still allow you to register and sit for your exam, but you will not receive your scores. Therefore, you should not proceed with this Step 3 until you have completed Step 2 above. You can complete both at the same time.

    b.   Once you have your Certification Entrance Fee in your shopping cart, click the "Certification" link from the left navigation menu. From there, click the "Register for an Exam" link.

    c.   Choose the exam part and testing window for which you would like to register and click "Add to Cart."

    d.   The system gives you a chance to add a registration for a second part in the same or different testing window. If you would like to add another part, repeat Step c. above. If you only want to take one part at this time, click the link that says "check out."

    e.   Your shopping cart may show the red box saying "Additional Information Required." Click on the alert to proceed to the Confidentiality Agreement, which you must read and check. Click "Finish" on this screen to proceed back to your shopping cart.

    f.   Now, you will see that you have a BLUE box with the words "ready for checkout."

    g.   You will now need to fill out your payment information. Then, click "Process My Order."

    h.   You will be taken to an "Order Summary" page with your order number and all relevant order information. You should print this page for your records. In addition, you will immediately receive a payment confirmation email and a "CMA Exam Authorization Letter" email. You should read and save both emails. If the Authorization Letter indicates that you need to take any kind of action (e.g., submit education credentials, etc.), you should do so immediately.

4.   Schedule your exam at Prometric.

    a.   Go to www.prometric.com/ICMA and click the "Schedule My Test" button to begin scheduling your exam.

    b.   You will then be asked to specify the country you would like to test in. Those in the United States will also need to specify a testing state from the drop-down box. You may proceed to the next step by clicking the "Next" button.

    c.   You will now be at the "Information Review" section of the scheduling process. This section contains pertinent information such as: "How to Become Eligible," "What to bring to the Testing Center," "What Time to Arrive at the Testing Center," "Payment," "Reschedule/Cancel Policy," and "Scheduling Online." Gleim encourages you to read this information, as it may bring to your attention information you were unaware of. You may continue on to Prometric's "Privacy Policy Review" by clicking the "Next" button.

    d.   Read Prometric's "Privacy Policy Review" page and click "I agree," then click "Next."

    e.   Enter your authorization number found on your CMA Exam Authorization Letter email, then enter the first four letters of your last name into the provided field. Click "Next."

    f.   Now, follow the on-screen prompts to navigate through locating and choosing a testing center, and choosing the date and time for your exam.

    g.   Review your appointment details to ensure that you have the correct time, date, and location for your test before you finalize your registration. If all information is correct and you wish to complete this registration, click the provided "Complete Registration" button.

    h.   The final screen provides you with a confirmation number as well as information on canceling and/or rescheduling your appointment. Additionally, you should receive an email within the next few hours with a summary of your appointment information.

1.14 MAINTAINING YOUR CMA DESIGNATION

When you have completed all requirements, you will be issued a numbered CMA certificate. This certificate is the property of the ICMA and must be returned upon request. To maintain your certificate, membership in the IMA is required. The annual CMA maintenance fee for regular members is $30. You are also required to comply with the IMA's *Statement of Ethical Professional Practice* and all applicable state laws. The final requirement is continuing professional education (CPE).

Beginning the calendar year after successful completion of the CMA exams, 30 hours of CPE must be completed, which is about 4 days per year. Qualifying topics include management accounting, corporate taxation, statistics, computer science, systems analysis, management skills, marketing, business law, and insurance. All CMAs are required to complete 2 hours of CPE on the subject of ethics as part of their 30-hour annual requirement.

1.15 ELIGIBILITY PERIOD

Candidates must register for an exam part within the first 12 months after being admitted to the Certification Program. In addition, all candidates are required to pass both parts of the exam within 3 years of being admitted to the CMA program. If a candidate is not able to pass both parts within this time period, the Certification Entrance Fee will have to be repaid and the passed part will have to be retaken.

1.16 THE GLEIM SYSTEM FOR CMA EXAM SUCCESS

The following is an abbreviated description of the information that is covered throughout the rest of this booklet.

The Preparation Process -- In order to be successful on examinations, you need to undertake the following steps:

1. Understand the exam, including its purpose, coverage, preparation, format, administration, and grading.

2. Learn and understand the subject matter tested.

3. Practice answering exam questions to perfect your exam-answering techniques.

4. Plan and practice exam execution.

5. Develop confidence and ensure success with a controlled preparation program followed by confident execution and control during the examination.

1.17 THE GLEIM CMA REVIEW TABLE OF CONTENTS

CMA REVIEW TABLE OF CONTENTS	
Part 1: Financial Reporting, Planning, Performance, and Control 1. External Financial Statements and Revenue Recognition 2. Measurement, Valuation, and Disclosure: Investments and Short-Term Items 3. Measurement, Valuation, and Disclosure: Long-Term Items 4. Cost Management Concepts 5. Cost Accumulation Systems 6. Cost Allocation Techniques 7. Operational Efficiency and Business Process Performance 8. Analysis and Forecasting Techniques 9. Budgeting – Concepts, Methodologies, and Preparation 10. Cost and Variance Measures 11. Responsibility Accounting and Performance Measures 12. Internal Controls – Risk and Procedures for Control 13. Internal Controls – Internal Auditing and Systems Controls	**Part 2: Financial Decision Making** 1. Ethics for Management Accountants 2. Ratio Analysis 3. Profitability Analysis and Analytical Issues 4. Investment Risk and Portfolio Management 5. Financial Instruments and Cost of Capital 6. Managing Current Assets 7. Raising Capital, Corporate Restructuring, and International Finance 8. CVP Analysis and Marginal Analysis 9. Decision Analysis and Risk Management 10. Investment Decisions

1.18 OTHER CMA REVIEW MATERIALS, SYSTEMS, AND COURSES

Gleim has been helping accountants pass the CMA exam since 1980! We have the experience and knowledge to help you pass the first time.

There are many other CMA Review providers. We, of course, want you to be successful with Gleim, but we recognize that you will look at alternative methods and products and may well use one or more CMA products in conjunction with Gleim to prepare for the CMA exam.

A major distinction is group study vs. self study. The Gleim system is self-study (unless you use our Professor-Led Live Review; see below). Group study is assembling with others to obtain live instruction, audio, and/or video lectures. Make sure that your instructor of such a course is a professor or someone who passed the CMA exam the first time, not just a PR person who merely turns a recorded lecture on or off!

The Gleim Professor-Led Live Review is ideal if you prefer group study. This program provides personalized and individual attention within a group dynamic. The Professor-Led Live Review provides you with a live weekly meeting with a professor, the Gleim Review System, a supportive online community with chatrooms and calendars, and access to Gleim Personal Counselors. Visit www.gleim.com/MoreCMA.

When looking at other materials, keep the following advice in mind:

1. AVOID being distracted by advertised pass rates. The reported percentage may be that for first-time candidates, all candidates, candidates passing a specific part of the examination, candidates passing both parts of the exam, or even candidates successfully passing the exam after a specified number of sittings.

2. AVOID the compulsion to overprepare. Your objective is to **pass** the exam. Virtually no one is ever going to ask you your exam scores. Many candidates invest time and money in multiple courses that contribute only marginally to their effort.

3. AVOID being sold on predictions of the specific topics to be tested on the next exam. The ICMA publishes the same Content Specification Outlines to all CMA review providers and candidates. Focusing on certain topics and excluding others based on predictions is NOT a sound strategy.

 Together, Gleim and the Institute of Management Accountants are focused on helping CMA candidates achieve success by ensuring that they pass the CMA Exam and have the knowledge and skills desired by the management accounting profession. Through this strategic partnership, we demonstrate our commitment to CMA candidates.

STUDY UNIT TWO
ICMA CONTENT SPECIFICATION OUTLINES

(8 pages of outline)

In this study unit, we have reproduced verbatim the ICMA's Content Specification Outlines (CSOs) for the CMA exam (found at www.imanet.org/PDFs/Public/CMA/CMA_CSO_2015.pdf), which are organized in outline format with areas, groups, and topics. There is a separate CSO for each part of the exam. Note the ICMA "percentage coverage," e.g., 20%, for each area. All Gleim CMA materials take these percentages into account to facilitate your study, learning, and success.

Candidates are responsible for being informed on the most recent developments in the areas covered in the outlines, including understanding public pronouncements issued by accounting organizations as well as being up-to-date on recent developments reported in current accounting, financial, and business periodicals.

2.1 OVERVIEW OF CSOs AND LEVELS OF COVERAGE

The ICMA has indicated five uses for the Content Specification Outlines:

1. Establish the foundation from which each examination will be developed.

2. Provide a basis for consistent coverage on each examination.

3. Communicate to interested parties more detail as to the content of each examination part.

4. Assist candidates in their preparation for each examination.

5. Provide information to those who offer courses designed to aid candidates in preparing for the examinations.

In addition to the CSOs, the ICMA provides Learning Outcome Statements (LOSs). The LOSs are more specific and describe in greater detail what the candidate needs to know about each section of the CSOs. Gleim materials cover these LOSs thoroughly. Also, for your convenience, we provide a reproduction of the relevant LOSs in each study unit of CMA Gleim Online.

Gleim Pass the CMA Video Series

Are you just starting to study for the CMA exam, or are you an experienced exam veteran? No matter what your skill level is, the Gleim "Pass the CMA Exam" video series can help launch your studies and give you tips on how to be successful!

www.gleim.com/CMAVideos

Levels of Coverage

According to the ICMA's Content Specification Outline document, "Each major topic within each examination part has been assigned a coverage level designating the depth and breadth of topic coverage, ranging from an introductory knowledge of a subject area (Level A) to a thorough understanding of and ability to apply the essentials of a subject area (Level C)." The ICMA's detailed explanations of the coverage levels and the skills expected of candidates are presented below.

The cognitive skills that a successful candidate should possess and that should be tested on the examination can be defined as follows:

Knowledge: Ability to remember previously learned material, such as specific facts, criteria, techniques, principles, and procedures (i.e., identify, define, list).

Comprehension: Ability to grasp and interpret the meaning of material (i.e., classify, explain, distinguish between).

Application: Ability to use learned material in new and concrete situations (i.e., demonstrate, predict, solve, modify, relate).

Analysis: Ability to break down material into its component parts so that its organizational structure can be understood; ability to recognize causal relationships, discriminate between behaviors, and identify elements that are relevant to the validation of a judgment (i.e., differentiate, estimate, order).

Synthesis: Ability to put parts together to form a new whole or proposed set of operations; ability to relate ideas and formulate hypotheses (i.e., combine, formulate, revise).

Evaluation: Ability to judge the value of material for a given purpose on the basis of consistency, logical accuracy, and comparison to standards; ability to appraise judgments involved in the selection of a course of action (i.e., criticize, justify, conclude).

The three levels of coverage can be defined as follows:

Level A: Requiring the skill levels of knowledge and comprehension.

Level B: Requiring the skill levels of knowledge, comprehension, application, and analysis.

Level C: Requiring all six skill levels, knowledge, comprehension, application, analysis, synthesis, and evaluation.

The levels of coverage as they apply to each of the major topics of the Content Specification Outlines are shown on the following pages with each topic listing. The levels represent the manner in which topic areas are to be treated and represent ceilings, i.e., a topic area designated as Level C may contain requirements at the "A," "B," or "C" level, but a topic designated as Level B will not contain requirements at the "C" level.

The Gleim CMA Review System is organized to ensure comprehensive coverage of the ICMA CSOs. Below and on the following pages, we have provided cross-references to our study units and subunits alongside the CSOs to facilitate your studying process. You can find the Table of Contents for the Gleim CMA Review material in Study Unit 1, Subunit 17.

2.2 CSO: PART 1 – FINANCIAL REPORTING, PLANNING, PERFORMANCE, AND CONTROL

A. **External Financial Reporting Decisions (15% - Levels A, B, and C)**

1. *Financial statements*

    a. Balance sheet (1.2)
    b. Income statement (1.3)
    c. Statement of changes in equity (1.4)
    d. Statement of cash flows (1.5)

2. *Recognition, measurement, valuation, and disclosure*

    a. Asset valuation (2.1-2.5, 3.1-3.4)
    b. Valuation of liabilities (2.8, 3.5-3.7)
    c. Equity transactions (2.7)
    d. Revenue recognition (1.6-1.7)
    e. Income measurement (1.6-1.7)
    f. Major differences between U.S. GAAP and IFRS (SU 1-SU 3)

B. **Planning, Budgeting, and Forecasting (30% - Levels A, B, and C)**

1. *Strategic Planning*

    a. Analysis of external and internal factors affecting strategy (SU 8)
    b. Long-term mission and goals (SU 8)
    c. Alignment of tactics with long-term strategic goals (SU 8)
    d. Strategic planning models and analytical techniques (8.1-8.5)
    e. Characteristics of successful strategic planning process (8.6-8.8)

2. *Budgeting concepts*

    a. Operations and performance goals (9.1)
    b. Characteristics of a successful budget process (9.1)
    c. Resource allocation (9.1)
    d. Other budgeting concepts (9.2)

3. *Forecasting techniques*

    a. Regression analysis (8.1)
    b. Learning curve analysis (8.2)
    c. Expected value (8.4)

4. *Budgeting methodologies*

    a. Annual business plans (master budgets) (9.3)
    b. Project budgeting (9.4)
    c. Activity-based budgeting (9.4)
    d. Zero-based budgeting (9.4)
    e. Continuous (rolling) budgets (9.4)
    f. Flexible budgeting (10.2)

5. *Annual profit plan and supporting schedules*

    a. Operational budgets (9.5-9.6)
    b. Financial budgets (9.7-9.8)
    c. Capital budgets (9.3)

6. *Top-level planning and analysis*

    a. Pro forma income (9.9)
    b. Financial statement projections (9.9)
    c. Cash flow projections (9.9)

C. Performance Management (20% - Levels A, B, and C)

1. *Cost and variance measures*

    a. Comparison of actual to planned results (10.1)
    b. Use of flexible budgets to analyze performance (10.2)
    c. Management by exception (10.1)
    d. Use of standard cost systems (10.2)
    e. Analysis of variation from standard cost expectations (10.3-10.8)

2. *Responsibility centers and reporting segments*

    a. Types of responsibility centers (11.1)
    b. Transfer pricing models (11.6-11.7)
    c. Reporting of organizational segments (11.2-11.3)

3. *Performance measures*

    a. Product profitability analysis (11.2)
    b. Business unit profitability analysis (11.2)
    c. Customer profitability analysis (11.2)
    d. Return on investment (11.3-11.4)
    e. Residual income (11.3-11.4)
    f. Investment base issues (11.3-11.4)
    g. Key performance indicators (KPIs) (8.7)
    h. Balanced scorecard (8.7)

D. Cost Management (20% - Levels A, B, and C)

1. *Measurement concepts*

    a. Cost behavior and cost objects (4.1-4.3)
    b. Actual and normal costs (4.4, 6.4-6.5)
    c. Standard costs (4.4, 6.4-6.5)
    d. Absorption (full) costing (6.1-6.2)
    e. Variable (direct) costing (6.1-6.2)
    f. Joint and by-product costing (6.3)

2. *Costing systems*

    a. Job order costing (5.1)
    b. Process costing (5.2)
    c. Activity-based costing (5.3)
    d. Life-cycle costing (5.4)

3. *Overhead costs*

    a. Fixed and variable overhead expenses (6.4-6.5)
    b. Plant-wide versus departmental overhead (6.4)
    c. Determination of allocation base (6.4-6.5)
    d. Allocation of service department costs (6.6-6.7)

4. **Supply Chain Management**

    a. Lean manufacturing (7.1)
    b. Enterprise resource planning (ERP) (7.2)
    c. Theory of constraints and throughput costing (7.3)
    d. Capacity management and analysis (7.4)

5. **Business process improvement**

    a. Value chain analysis (7.5)
    b. Value-added concepts (7.5)
    c. Process analysis (7.6)
    d. Activity-based management (5.3,7.6)
    e. Continuous improvement concepts (5.3, 7.6)
    f. Best practice analysis (7.6)
    g. Cost of quality analysis (7.6)
    h. Efficient accounting processes (7.6)

E. **Internal Controls (15 - Levels A, B, and C)**

    1. **Governance, risk, and compliance**

        a. Internal control structure and management philosophy (12.1)
        b. Internal control policies for safeguarding and assurance (12.2)
        c. Internal control risk (12.1-12.2)
        d. Corporate governance (12.3)
        e. External audit requirements (12.3)

    2. **Internal auditing**

        a. Responsibility and authority of the internal audit function (13.1)
        b. Types of audits conducted by internal auditors (13.1)

    3. **System controls and security measures**

        a. General accounting system controls (13.2)
        b. Application and transaction controls (13.2)
        c. Network controls (13.3)
        d. Backup controls (13.3)
        e. Business continuity planning (13.3)

2.3 CSO: PART 2 – FINANCIAL DECISION MAKING

A. **Financial Statement Analysis (25% - Levels A, B, and C)**

    1. **Basic Financial Statement Analysis**

        a. Common size financial statements (3.8)
        b. Common base year financial statements (3.8)

    2. **Financial Ratios**

        a. Liquidity (2.1-2.2)
        b. Leverage (2.5)
        c. Activity (2.3)
        d. Profitability (3.1-3.2)
        e. Market (3.3)

3. *Profitability analysis*

   a. Income measurement analysis (3.6)
   b. Revenue analysis (3.6)
   c. Cost of sales analysis (3.6)
   d. Expense analysis (3.6)
   e. Variation analysis (3.6)

4. *Special Issues*

   a. Impact of foreign operations (3.7)
   b. Effects of changing prices and inflation (3.5)
   c. Off-balance sheet financing (3.9)
   d. Impact of changes in accounting treatment (3.6)
   e. Accounting and economic concepts of value and income (8.5)
   f. Earnings quality (3.5)

B. **Corporate Finance (20% - Levels A, B, and C)**

   1. *Risk and return*

      a. Calculating return (4.1)
      b. Types of risk (4.1)
      c. Relationship between risk and return (4.1)

   2. *Long-term financial management*

      a. Term structure of interest rates (5.1)
      b. Types of financial instruments (5.1-5.2, 5.4)
      c. Cost of capital (5.6-5.7)
      d. Valuation of financial instruments (5.3-5.4)

   3. *Raising capital*

      a. Financial markets and regulation (7.1)
      b. Market efficiency (7.1)
      c. Financial institutions (7.1)
      d. Initial and secondary public offerings (7.1)
      e. Dividend policy and share repurchases (7.2)
      f. Lease financing (7.2)

   4. *Working capital management*

      a. Working capital terminology (6.1)
      b. Cash management (6.2)
      c. Marketable securities management (6.3)
      d. Accounts receivable management (6.4)
      e. Inventory management (6.5)
      f. Types of short-term credit (6.6)
      g. Short-term credit management (6.6)

   5. *Corporate restructuring*

      a. Mergers and acquisitions (7.3)
      b. Bankruptcy (7.4)
      c. Other forms of restructuring (7.3)

   6. *International finance*

      a. Fixed, flexible, and floating exchange rates (7.5)
      b. Managing transaction exposure (7.6)
      c. Financing international trade (7.7)
      d. Tax implications of transfer pricing (7.7)

C. **Decision Analysis (20% - Levels A, B, and C)**

  1. *Cost/volume/profit analysis*

    a. Breakeven analysis (8.1-8.2)
    b. Profit performance and alternative operating levels (8.3)
    c. Analysis of multiple products (8.4)

  2. *Marginal analysis*

    a. Sunk costs, opportunity costs and other related concepts (8.5)
    b. Marginal costs and marginal revenue (8.5-8.6)
    c. Special orders and pricing (9.2)
    d. Make versus buy (9.3)
    e. Sell or process further (9.4)
    f. Add or drop a segment (9.1)
    g. Capacity considerations (9.1-9.4)

  3. *Pricing*

    a. Pricing methodologies (9.6)
    b. Target costing (9.6-9.7)
    c. Elasticity of demand (9.5)
    d. Product life cycle considerations (9.6)
    e. Market structure considerations (9.6)

D. **Risk Management (10% - Levels A, B, and C)**

  1. *Enterprise risk*

    a. Types of risk (9.8)
    b. Risk identification and assessment (9.8)
    c. Risk mitigation strategies (9.8)
    d. Managing risk (9.8)

E. **Investment Decisions (15% - Levels A, B, and C)**

  1. *Capital budgeting process*

    a. Stages of capital budgeting (10.1)
    b. Incremental cash flows (10.1)
    c. Income tax considerations (10.1)

  2. *Discounted cash flow analysis*

    a. Net present value (10.2, 10.5)
    b. Internal rate of return (10.2, 10.5)
    c. Comparison of NPV and IRR (10.2, 10.5)

  3. *Payback and discounted payback*

    a. Uses of payback method (10.3, 10.5)
    b. Limitations of payback method (10.3, 10.5)
    c. Discounted payback (10.3, 10.5)

  4. *Risk analysis in capital investment*

    a. Sensitivity and scenario analysis (10.6)
    b. Real options (10.6)

F. **Professional Ethics (10% - Levels A, B, and C)**

1. ***Ethical considerations for management accounting and financial management professionals***

    a. IMA's "Statement of Ethical Professional Practice" (1.1)
    b. Fraud triangle (1.4)
    c. Evaluation and resolution of ethical issues (1.1-1.3)

2. ***Ethical considerations for the organization***

    a. IMA's Statement on Management Accounting, "Values and Ethics: From Inception to Practice" (1.2)
    b. U.S. Foreign Corrupt Practices Act (1.2)
    c. Corporate responsibility for ethical conduct (1.2-1.3)

STUDY UNIT THREE
CONTENT PREPARATION, TEST ADMINISTRATION, AND PERFORMANCE GRADING

(2 pages of outline)

This study unit consists primarily of a detailed listing of procedures and rules used to administer the exam. Remember, the more you know about the examination process and what to expect, the bigger your competitive advantage over others taking the exam. Leave nothing to chance, and be in total control of the examination process.

3.1 THE NONDISCLOSED EXAM

The CMA is a **nondisclosed** exam. **Nondisclosed** means that exam questions and solutions are NOT released after each examination. As part of the ICMA's nondisclosure policy and to prove each candidate's willingness to adhere to this policy, a confidentiality agreement must be accepted by each candidate before each part is taken. This statement is reproduced here to remind all CMA candidates about the ICMA's strict policy of nondisclosure, which Gleim consistently supports and upholds.

> *I hereby attest that I will not divulge the content of this examination, nor will I remove any examination materials, notes or other unauthorized materials from the examination room. I understand that failure to comply with this attestation may result in invalidation of my grades and disqualification from future examinations. For those already certified by the Institute of Certified Management Accountants, failure to comply with the statement will be considered a violation of the IMA's Statement of Ethical Professional Practice and could result in revocation of the certification.*

3.2 ICMA BOARD OF REGENTS

The ICMA was created out of the IMA to develop and administer the CMA exam. Specifically, the ICMA's Board of Regents, a panel of management accounting and financial management experts, oversees the exam. The Board, along with the ICMA staff, evaluates the program's applicants to ensure their credentials meet the requirements. It also develops and updates the content of the exam to ensure it aligns with a general body of knowledge that all practicing management accountants should possess and be able to implement on a daily basis. The Board then administers and grades the exams, and it remains involved with candidates past certification by running the continuing education program for CMAs.

3.3 WHICH PRONOUNCEMENTS ARE TESTED?

New pronouncements are eligible to be tested on the CMA exam in the testing window beginning 1 year after a pronouncement's effective date.

3.4 HOW ETHICS ARE TESTED

Ethical issues and considerations will be tested from the perspective of the individual in Part 1 and from the perspective of the organization in Part 2. Candidates will be expected to evaluate the issues involved and make recommendations for the resolution of the situation.

3.5 PRETESTING QUESTIONS

The ICMA pretests an undisclosed number of multiple-choice questions on each exam part. These questions do not count toward your final grade. You will not know which are "pretest" questions and thus must answer each question as if it will be graded.

3.6 GRADING AND SCORE REPORT

You will not receive immediate pass/fail results on your CMA exam because the essays must be graded offline at a later time. The ICMA will mail you your scores approximately 6 weeks from the end of the month in which you took the exam. Candidates with failing grades will receive a Performance Feedback Report detailing the content area(s) in which the candidate needs improvement.

The essays are worth 25% of the total exam score, and the multiple-choice section is worth 75%. The scores for the multiple-choice section will be added to the scores of the essay section for a total weighted score of pass/fail reflected in a scaled score for the entire part. You MUST score at least 50% on the multiple-choice section of the exam to be allowed to take the essay section. This requirement ensures that test takers do not proceed with the essay section if they do not have a chance of achieving a passing score for the entire exam. If you are allowed to proceed, it does not mean that you passed. You still must perform well enough on the essay section of the exam to achieve a total passing score.

Candidates are given different "forms" of the exam, and each form must have a passing score that takes into consideration its relative difficulty. Therefore, the scores for each part are placed along a scale from 0 to 500, and candidates need a score of at least 360 to pass.

3.7 PASS RATES

	May 1, 2013 – February 28, 2014*
Part 1 – Financial Planning, Performance, and Control	35%
Part 2 – Financial Decision Making	42%

A major difference among CMA candidates is their preparation program. You have access to the best CMA review material; it is up to you to use it. Conversely, if you do not apply the suggestions in this booklet, *How to Pass the CMA Exam: A System for Success*, you will be at a disadvantage to the thousands of candidates who will pass with Gleim. Even if you are enrolled in a review course that uses other manuals, you will benefit with the Gleim CMA Review System. Compare our products to theirs and understand why Gleim has helped more CMA candidates than any other program.

NOTE: These pass rates are worldwide.

*For any more recent pass rates, check our website at www.gleim.com/BecomeCMA.

STUDY UNIT FOUR
MULTIPLE-CHOICE QUESTIONS

(8 pages of outline)

This study unit ("Multiple-Choice Questions") and Study Unit 5 ("Essay Questions") explain question formats that appear on the CMA exam. We also suggest time-budgeting and question-answering techniques for each.

You will probably recognize that your question-answering technique is a specific control system application. We cannot say that your question-answering technique control system is more important than your other control systems, which include understanding the exam, studying individual Gleim study units, and planning and practicing exam execution. You will, however, be confident about your performance on the CMA exam when you are poised to maximize your points on every question.

4.1 EXAM FORMAT RECAP

There are two parts to the CMA exam.

Part 1: Financial Reporting, Planning, Performance, and Control
Part 2: Financial Decision Making

Each part consists of 100 multiple-choice questions and two essay questions. The multiple-choice questions will be delivered in random order, meaning that the order of questions will not reflect the order in which the topics are presented in the CSOs. Four hours is allowed for the completion of an entire part (3 hours for the multiple-choice, 1 hour for the essays). If you complete your 100 multiple-choice questions by allocating 1.5 minutes per question, you will have 30 minutes to review. Use as much of this time to review as you need, and then move on to the essays. Your unused multiple-choice section time will be carried over to the essay section and added on to the hour time allocation.

Do not be surprised or flustered if you end up with more or less than 30 minutes left on the time remaining clock when you have finished all 100 of your multiple-choice questions. If you have more than 30 minutes, do a thorough review of your marked questions, make sure you have answered all 100 questions, and move on to the essays knowing you have plenty of time.

If you finish with less than 30 minutes, do not panic. Remain calm and in control. Make sure you have answered all 100 questions (make educated guesses if you need to) and move on to the essays. One hour is certainly enough to answer both questions -- you're doing fine! See the rest of this study unit and Study Unit 7, Subunit 9, for more information on time-budgeting and question-answering techniques for the multiple-choice section.

Conceptual vs. Calculation Questions

Some CMA exam questions will be calculations in contrast to conceptual questions. When you take the test, it may appear that more of the questions are calculation-type because they take longer and are more difficult.

See Study Unit 7, Subunit 6, for the calculators that the ICMA has approved for use on the CMA exam.

4.2 MULTIPLE-CHOICE QUESTIONS

Multiple-choice questions consist of a stem (the question) and four answer choices. One answer is correct, and three answer choices are incorrect. Another view is that there is one answer choice that is the best response to the question stem. Two CMA multiple-choice questions appear below.

Part 1

1. Which one of the following **best** describes direct labor?

   A.   A prime cost.

   B.   A period cost.

   C.   A product cost.

   D.   Both a product cost and a prime cost.

Part 2

2. Hi-Tech, Inc., has determined that it can minimize its weighted average cost of capital (WACC) by using a debt-equity ratio of 2/3. If the firm's cost of debt is 9% before taxes, the cost of equity is estimated to be 12% before taxes, and the tax rate is 40%, what is the firm's WACC?

   A.   6.48%

   B.   7.92%

   C.   9.36%

   D.   10.80%

Some multiple-choice questions contain words like *except*, *not*, *unless*, *least*, etc., as illustrated below.

Which of the following is **not** a method of financing international trade?

All of the following statements in regard to working capital are true **except**

These negative stems ask for the false answer choice, which is accompanied by three true answer choices. Expect a few multiple-choice questions with negative stems on the exam. Presumably, the ICMA will print these **negative** words in bold type, as illustrated above.

4.3 LESS TRADITIONAL MULTIPLE-CHOICE QUESTIONS

Other types of multiple-choice questions include

1. Questions with two or three answer options
2. Questions with two, three, or four variables in each answer
3. Graphic representations

Occasionally, the ICMA converts two- and three-answer multiple-choice questions into four-answer multiple-choice questions. Mark each of the I, II, III, and IVs as true or false.

3. Mega, Inc., a large conglomerate with operating divisions in many industries, uses risk-adjusted discount rates in evaluating capital investment decisions. Consider the following statements concerning Mega's use of risk-adjusted discount rates.

I.   Mega may accept some investments with internal rates of return less than Mega's overall average cost of capital.

II.   Discount rates vary depending on the type of investment.

III.   Mega may reject some investments with internal rates of return greater than the cost of capital.

IV.   Discount rates may vary depending on the division.

Which of the above statements are **correct**?

   A.   I and III only.

   B.   II and IV only.

   C.   II, III, and IV only.

   D.   I, II, III, and IV.

Other multiple-choice questions have several variables (or answers) within each answer option and are presented in columns. Circle the correct answer in each column.

4. The costing method that is properly classified for both external and internal reporting purposes is

		External Reporting	Internal Reporting
A.	Activity-based costing	No	Yes
B.	Job-order costing	No	Yes
C.	Variable costing	No	Yes
D.	Process costing	No	No

Yet other questions require various graphical interpretation, as illustrated in question 5 below.

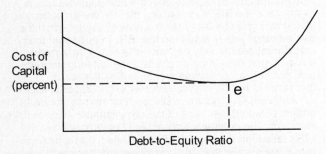

5. In referring to the graph of a firm's cost of capital, if e is the optimal position, which one of the following statements **best** explains the saucer or U-shaped curve?

A. The composition of debt and equity does not affect the firm's cost of capital.

B. The cost of capital is almost always favorably influenced by increases in financial leverage.

C. The cost of capital is almost always negatively influenced by increases in financial leverage.

D. Use of at least some debt financing will enhance the value of the firm.

The answer explanations for the sample questions appear on the next page.

4.4 ANSWER EXPLANATIONS

1. Answer (D) is correct.
REQUIRED: The best description of direct labor.
DISCUSSION: Direct labor is both a product cost and a prime cost. Product costs are incurred to produce units of output and are deferred to future periods to the extent that output is not sold. Prime costs are defined as direct materials and direct labor.
Answer (A) is incorrect. Direct labor is also a product cost. Answer (B) is incorrect. A period cost is expensed when incurred. Direct labor cost is inventoriable. Answer (C) is incorrect. Direct labor is also a prime cost.

2. Answer (C) is correct.
REQUIRED: The firm's weighted-average cost of capital.
DISCUSSION: A firm's weighted-average cost of capital (WACC) is derived by weighting the (after-tax) cost of each component of the financing structure by its proportion of the financing structure as a whole. Hi-Tech's WACC can be calculated as follows:

Component	Weight		Component Cost		Totals
Debt	40%	×	5.4%	=	2.16%
Equity	60%	×	12.0%	=	7.20%
					9.36%

$$\text{WACC} = 9.36\% = \left(\frac{3}{5} \times 12\%\right) + \left\{\frac{2}{5} \times \left[9\% \times (1 - 0.4)\right]\right\}$$

Answer (A) is incorrect. Improperly subtracting the effect of taxes from the cost of equity results in 6.48%. Answer (B) is incorrect. Improperly subtracting the effect of taxes from equity, but not from debt, results in 7.92%. Answer (D) is incorrect. Improperly using the before-tax cost of debt results in 10.80%.

3. Answer (D) is correct.
REQUIRED: The true statement about use of risk-adjusted discount rates.
DISCUSSION: Risk analysis attempts to measure the likelihood of the variability of future returns from the proposed investment. Risk can be incorporated into capital budgeting decisions in a number of ways, one of which is to use a hurdle rate higher than the firm's cost of capital, that is, a risk-adjusted discount rate. This technique adjusts the interest rate used for discounting upward as an investment becomes riskier. The expected flow from the investment must be relatively larger, or the increased discount rate will generate a negative net present value, and the proposed acquisition will be rejected. Accordingly, the IRR (the rate at which the NPV is zero) for a rejected investment may exceed the cost of capital when the risk-adjusted rate is higher than the IRR. Conversely, the IRR for an accepted investment may be less than the cost of capital when the risk-adjusted rate is less than the IRR. In this case, the investment presumably has very little risk. Furthermore, risk-adjusted rates may also reflect the differing degrees of risk, not only among investments, but by the same investments undertaken by different organizational subunits.
Answer (A) is incorrect. Discount rates may vary with the project or with the subunit of the organization. Answer (B) is incorrect. The company may accept some projects with IRRs less than the cost of capital or reject some projects with IRRs greater than the cost of capital. Answer (C) is incorrect. The company may accept some projects with IRRs less than the cost of capital or reject some projects with IRRs greater than the cost of capital.

4. Answer (C) is correct.
REQUIRED: The costing method that is properly classified for both internal and external reporting purposes.
DISCUSSION: Activity-based costing, job-order costing, process costing, and standard costing can all be used for both internal and external purposes. Variable costing is not acceptable under GAAP for external reporting purposes.
Answer (A) is incorrect. ABC is appropriate for external as well as internal purposes. Answer (B) is incorrect. Job-order costing is acceptable for external reporting purposes. Answer (D) is incorrect. Process costing is acceptable for external reporting purposes.

5. Answer (D) is correct.
REQUIRED: The best explanation of the U-shaped curve in a cost-of-capital graph.
DISCUSSION: The U-shaped curve indicates that the cost of capital is quite high when the debt-to-equity ratio is quite low. As debt increases, the cost of capital declines as long as the cost of debt is less than that of equity. Eventually, the decline in the cost of capital levels off because the cost of debt ultimately rises as more debt is used. Additional increases in debt (relative to equity) will then increase the cost of capital. The implication is that some debt is present in the optimal capital structure because the cost of capital initially declines when debt is added. However, a point is reached (e) at which debt becomes excessive and the cost of capital begins to rise.
Answer (A) is incorrect. The composition of the capital structure affects the cost of capital since the components have different costs. Answer (B) is incorrect. The cost of debt does not remain constant as financial leverage increases. Eventually, that cost also increases. Answer (C) is incorrect. Increased leverage is initially favorable.

4.5 MULTIPLE-CHOICE QUESTION-ANSWERING TECHNIQUE

The following suggestions are to assist you in maximizing your score on each part of the CMA exam. Remember, knowing how to take the exam and how to answer individual questions is important while you study and review the subject matter tested.

1. **Budget your time.** We make this point with emphasis. Just as you would fill up your gas tank prior to reaching empty, so too would you finish your exam before time expires.

   a. You have 180 minutes to answer 100 questions, i.e., 1.8 minutes per question. We suggest you allocate 1.5 minutes per question. This would result in completing 100 questions in 150 minutes to give you 30 minutes to review your answers and questions that you have marked.

   b. On your Prometric computer screen, the time remaining (starting with 3:00:00) appears at the top right corner of your screen. See Study Unit 7, Subunit 9, for details on how to track your progress on the scratch paper Prometric will provide using hours:minutes.

2. **Answer the questions in consecutive order.**

   a. Do **not** agonize over any one item or question. Stay within your time budget.

   b. Mark any questions you are unsure of and return to them later as time allows. Plan on going back to all the questions you marked.

   c. Never leave a multiple-choice question unanswered. **Make your best educated guess in the time allowed.** Remember that your score is based on the number of correct responses. You will not be penalized for guessing incorrectly.

3. **For each multiple-choice question,**

   a. **Try to ignore the answer choices.** Do not allow the answer choices to affect your reading of the question.

      1) If four answer choices are presented, three of them are incorrect. They are called **distractors** for good reason. Often, distractors are written to appear correct at first glance until further analysis.

      2) In computational items, the distractors are carefully calculated such that they are the result of making common mistakes. Be careful, and double-check your computations if time permits.

   b. **Read the question carefully** to determine the precise requirement.

      1) Focusing on what is required enables you to ignore extraneous information, to focus on the relevant facts, and to proceed directly to determining the correct answer.

         a) Be especially careful to note when the requirement is an **exception**; e.g., "All of the following statements regarding a company's internal rate of return are true **except**:"

   c. **Determine the correct answer** before looking at the answer choices.

   d. **Read the answer choices carefully.**

      1) Even if the first answer appears to be the correct choice, do **not** skip the remaining answer choices. Questions often ask for the "best" of the choices provided. Thus, each choice requires your consideration.

      2) Treat each answer choice as a true/false question as you analyze it.

e.   **Click on the best answer.**

1)   You have a 25% chance of answering the question correctly by blindly guessing; improve your odds with educated guessing.

2)   For many multiple-choice questions, two answer choices can be eliminated with minimal effort, thereby increasing your educated guess to a 50-50 proposition.

4.   After completing your first pass through all 100 questions, return to the questions that you marked.

5.   Remember to stay on schedule. Time control is critical.

4.6 EDUCATED GUESSING

The CMA exam often includes questions that are poorly worded or confusing. Expect the unexpected and move forward. Educated guessing is a must. When you encounter such a question on the exam, do not let it affect your concentration or take up too much time. Use your best guess and move on. Gleim will continue to improve review material based on customer feedback and information releases from the test administrator.

If you don't know the answer, make an educated guess. First, rule out answers that you feel are obviously incorrect. Second, speculate on the ICMA's purpose and/or the rationale behind the question. Third, select the best answer or guess between equally appealing answers. Mark the question by clicking on the "Mark" button in case you have time to return to it for further analysis. However, unless you made an obvious mistake or computational error, try to avoid changing answers at the last minute. Your first guess is usually the most intuitive.

If you cannot make an educated guess, pick the most intuitive answer. Never leave a question unanswered.

NOTE: Our recommendation to aid you in perfecting educated guessing is to take multiple-choice and true/false quizzes in CMA Gleim Online BEFORE YOU STUDY EACH STUDY UNIT. See "How to Use the Gleim Review System" on page 37.

4.7 MULTIPLE-CHOICE TIME BUDGETING AND CONTROL WITH GLEIM PRACTICE EXAMS

Using the Gleim study system, you will do a minimum of two 20-question Practice Exams for each study unit to help you answer multiple-choice questions in 1.5 minutes each. See Study Unit 7, Subunit 9, for more information on time budgeting. Practice makes perfect!

Live by and thrive on 20-question Practice Exams. We use 20-question Exams because they are of sufficient length to work you but are not too long. Based on decades of experience, we are very confident recommending and using 20-question Exams. You will have no trouble budgeting your time on the CMA exam after extensive practice with 20-question Exams.

Each Practice Exam should be completed in 30 minutes (plus 10 minutes for review) under exam conditions. Practice marking questions you wish to return to, but select the best answer for each question on your first pass.

It is imperative that you review each question you marked and/or answered incorrectly after you have completed each Exam. Analyze and understand why you answered each question incorrectly. This step is an essential learning activity because you learn more from each question of which you were unsure or answered incorrectly than from questions answered correctly. In other words, you learn from your mistakes, as we all do. It is important to learn and understand the subject matter tested and how to answer questions when you are unsure of the correct answer.

Learning from Your Mistakes

Learning from questions you answer incorrectly is very important. Each question you answer incorrectly is an **opportunity** to avoid missing actual test questions on your CMA exam. Thus, you should carefully study the answer explanations provided until you understand why the original answer you chose is wrong, as well as why the correct answer indicated is correct. This study technique is clearly the difference between passing and failing for many CMA candidates.

Also, you **must** determine why you answered questions incorrectly and learn how to avoid the same error in the future. Reasons for missing questions include

1. Misreading the requirement (stem)
2. Not understanding what is required
3. Making a math error
4. Applying the wrong rule or concept
5. Being distracted by one or more of the answers
6. Incorrectly eliminating answers from consideration
7. Not having any knowledge of the topic tested
8. Employing bad intuition when guessing

It is also important to verify that you answered correctly for the right reasons. Otherwise, if the material is tested on the CMA exam in a different manner, you may not answer it correctly.

4.8   TOOLBAR ICONS AND NAVIGATION

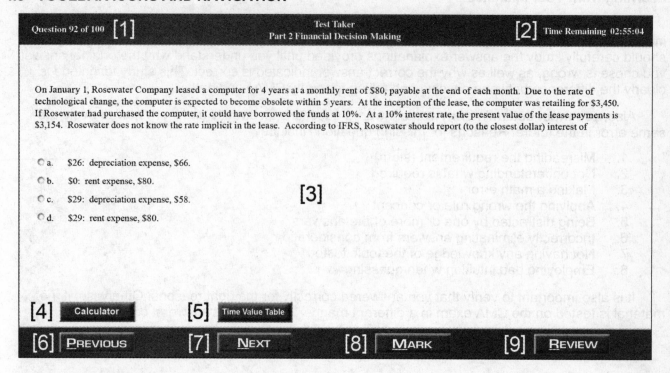

1. Question Number: The question number indicates which question the candidate is answering out of the total questions.

2. Time Remaining: This information box displays to the candidate how long (s)he has remaining to complete and review the multiple-choice questions. Consistently check the amount of time remaining in order to stay on schedule.

3. Question: This section displays the content of the current question the candidate is answering. Click an answer choice to select it.

4. Calculator: The calculator provided is a basic tool for simple computations. It is similar to calculators used in common software programs.

5. Time Value Tables: This function allows the candidate to access Present/Future Time Value Tables as needed.

6. Previous: This navigation button allows the candidate to move back to the previous question.

7. Next: This navigation button allows the candidate to move ahead to the next question.

8. Mark: This button allows the candidate to mark a question for later review.

9. Review: Clicking this button takes the candidate to the Review screen, which contains a scrollable listing of all the question numbers and indicates if the question has been marked for review, completed, or skipped.

USE GLEIM CMA TEST PREP and GLEIM ONLINE. They emulate the Prometric testing procedures and environment, including computer screen layout, software operation, etc.

STUDY UNIT FIVE
ESSAY QUESTIONS

(5 pages of outline)

5.1 CMA ESSAY QUESTIONS

Each part of the CMA exam contains two essays. You have at least 1 hour to complete both. If you finish your multiple-choice questions section in less than 3 hours, your remaining time will be carried over to the essay section and added to the standard 1-hour allocation. See Subunit 4 of this study unit for more information on essay time budgeting and control.

The written-response questions will not be graded online. Instead, the questions will be graded by subject matter experts, and partial credit will be given. For example, if you are asked to give three reasons why a selected alternative action is good for a business and you provide only two correct reasons, you will receive partial credit for these two responses. Likewise, for questions requiring a calculated response, partial credit will be given for a correct formula even though a mathematical error may have been made in the final number. In addition, you should include everything you know about a topic, even if you do not have a good grasp on the main topic. You may receive points for extraneous information because it shows you know a lot about the general subject.

The ICMA grades candidates on both subject matter and writing skills on the essay portion of the CMA exam. For writing skills to be graded, the response must be relevant to the question asked. The specific criteria for the ICMA's grading are as follows:

- Use of standard English – includes proper grammar, punctuation, and spelling.
- Organization – response is arranged logically and coherently.
- Clarity – analysis is clearly communicated with well-constructed sentences and appropriate vocabulary.

Gleim "Pass the CMA Exam" Video Series

Does studying for the essay portion of the CMA exam have you stressed? Get the answers to all your questions about this crucial part, along with other tips on how to be successful, in the Gleim "Pass the CMA Exam" video series!

www.gleim.com/CMAVideos

5.2 ESSAY INSTRUCTIONS

It is important to become familiar with the information below and on the following pages so that you can spend more of your time focusing on the content of the exam rather than on the format. We have added screenshots of Prometric-emulating essay questions to better prepare you for how the exam will look.

The following example shows a typical essay question:

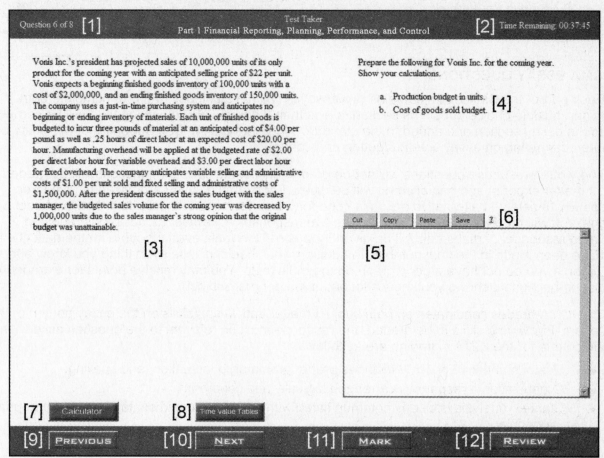

1. Question Number: The question number indicates which question the candidate is answering out of the total questions in both scenarios.

2. Time Remaining: This information box displays to the candidate how long (s)he has remaining to complete and review the essays. Consistently check the amount of time remaining in order to stay on schedule.

3. Scenario: This section displays the content of the current essay's scenario.

4. Question: This section displays the content of the current question the candidate is answering.

5. Answer Box: This area is where the candidate types in his or her response to the current question.

6. Word Processing Tools: These icons, when selected, enable the candidate to cut, copy, paste, and save the content of his or her response (much like a standard word processing program).

7. Calculator: The calculator provided is a basic tool for simple computations. It is similar to calculators used in common software programs.

8. Time Value Tables: This function allows the candidate to access Present/Future Time Value Tables as needed.

9. Previous: This navigation button allows the candidate to move back to the previous question.

10. Next: This navigation button allows the candidate to move ahead to the next question.

11. Mark: This button allows the candidate to mark a question for later review.

12. Review: Clicking this button takes the candidate to the Review screen, which contains a scrollable listing of all the question numbers and indicates if the question has been marked for review, completed, or skipped.

5.3 SAVING AND REVIEWING

Saving Your Response

Clicking on "Save" stores what you have typed in response to the current question. It is recommended that you save your answer every 5 minutes. When you have finished answering the question, review your answer and make any final revisions. Once you are satisfied with your answer, click on "Save" to store this answer. Clicking on "Next" to move on to the next question will automatically save your completed response.

Reviewing Items

At the end of the exam, you will see a scrollable listing of all the question numbers. This list displays each question number and indicates if the question has been marked for review, completed, or skipped.

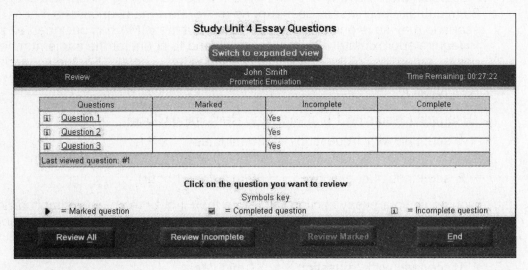

1. **To review questions**

    Click on the Review All button. You will be moved to the first question. Clicking on the Next button will cause you to move to the next question. You can also double-click on the question number in the list to move to a particular question.

2. **To review marked questions**

    Click on the Review Marked button. You will be moved to the first marked question. Clicking on the Next button will cause you to move to the next marked question.

3. **To review incomplete questions**

    Click on the Review Incomplete button. You will be moved to the first incomplete question. Clicking on the Next button will cause you to move to the next incomplete question.

5.4 ESSAY-ANSWERING TECHNIQUES

The Gleim essay questions in Gleim Online and Essay Wizard allow you to prepare for the essay section of your exam under true exam conditions. Each study unit in Gleim Online includes one essay scenario with multiple questions each. Each study unit in Essay Wizard contains at least two additional scenarios. After you grade each essay question, you should review the concepts that you marked and/or did not answer correctly. The objective is to determine why you missed each question in order to avoid making similar mistakes on the CMA exam.

Exam Tactics

The following tactical suggestions are to assist you in maximizing your score on the essay section of the CMA exam. Remember, knowing how to take the exam and how to answer individual questions is as important as studying the subject matter tested on the exam.

1. **Budget your time.**

   a. We make this point with emphasis. Just as you would fill up your gas tank prior to reaching empty, so too would you finish your exam before time expires.

   b. You have at least 1 hour to answer multiple questions based on two essay scenarios. If you finished your multiple-choice section in less than the allocated 3 hours, your remaining time will be carried over to the essay section and added to the 1-hour allocation.

   c. If you begin the essays with 1 hour on the Time Remaining Clock, you should allocate 30 minutes to each essay scenario, no matter how many questions it has. Each scenario may have one or more questions, but the ICMA has designed all scenarios to require approximately 30 minutes each and to count for the same number of points, regardless of the number of questions they contain. For the scenarios that contain more than one question, divide 30 minutes equally among the questions (see below).

   Example (assuming 1 hour on Time Remaining Clock):

1 scenario with 1 question	= 30 minutes
+1 scenario with 3 questions	= 30 minutes (10 minutes per question)
2 scenarios, 4 questions	= 60 minutes (1 hour)

   d. If you begin your essay section with more than 1 hour remaining, simply divide the time you have left in half and complete one essay scenario per half (see below).

   Example (assuming 1 hour, 15 minutes on Time Remaining Clock):

1 scenario with 1 question	= 37 minutes
+1 scenario with 3 questions	= 37 minutes (12 minutes per question)
2 scenarios, 4 questions	= 75 minutes (1 hour, 15 minutes)

   e. For more on essay time management, see Study Unit 7, Subunit 9.

2. **For each scenario, note the suggested time allocation (i.e., half your total time) and plan your response**.

   a. **Read requirements for each question carefully.**

      1) Focusing on what is required enables you to hone in on the relevant information.

   b. Allocate your time spent per question associated with each scenario by dividing your total time for that scenario equally among questions.

   c. On a sheet of scratch paper, outline the grading concepts for each of the requirements. Also note any related information you may be able to include to add to your points.

   d. Type your answers, proofread, and edit.

3. **Answer questions in sequential order.**

   a. Do **not** agonize over any one question or scenario. Stay within your time budget.

   b. As time permits, you can return to questions previously completed.

4. **Time is precious.** You will likely need the entire hour to answer all of the questions. Be prepared to stay at your Prometric computer for the entire time (i.e., no breaks).

GLEIM®

What makes us different?

☑ Materials written by experts

☑ Commitment to excellent customer care

☑ Tried and true review systems and study plans

☑ 40-year history of helping candidates pass their exams

☑ Gleim Instruct video series

Call **888.874.5346** or visit **gleim.com/GoCMA** to learn more

STUDY UNIT SIX
PREPARING TO PASS THE CMA EXAM

(6 pages of outline)

Preparing to sit for the CMA exam requires planning and control, i.e., a control system. This study unit suggests study and preparation procedures to maximize your test scores.

6.1 HOW TO BE IN CONTROL

You have to be in control to be successful during exam preparation and execution. Control is a process that we use in all our activities, implicitly or explicitly. The objective is to improve performance as well as be confident that the best possible performance is being generated. Control is a process whereby you

1. Develop expectations, standards, budgets, and plans.
2. Undertake activity, production, study, and learning.
3. Measure the activity, production, output, and knowledge.
4. Compare actual activity with expected and budgeted activity.
5. Modify the activity, behavior, or study to better achieve the desired outcome.
6. Revise expectations and standards in light of actual experience.
7. Continue the process or restart the process in the future.

Most accountants study this control process in relation to standard costs, i.e., establish cost standards and compute cost variances. Just as it helps them in their jobs, the control process will help you pass the CMA exam.

Unless you are a natural at something, most endeavors will improve with explicit control. This is particularly true with the CMA exam.

1. Develop an explicit control system over your study process.

2. Practice your question-answering techniques (and develop control) as you prepare solutions to practice questions/problems during your study program.

3. Plan to use the Gleim Time Management System (explained in Study Unit 7, Subunit 9) at the exam.

Also, notice the similarity of being prepared and being in control. Preparation is the key to success on the CMA exam: knowing what to expect and what to do to **pass the exam**! Control is exactly what *How to Pass the CMA Exam: A System for Success* and the other components of the Gleim Knowledge Transfer System give you.

6.2   DEVELOP YOUR STUDY PLAN

Remember that the exams are offered in three 2-month windows every year. Candidates should plan to complete both parts in 1 year.

The Gleim CMA Review program consists of 13 study units in Part 1 and 10 study units in Part 2, or a total of 23 study units for both parts of the exam. Complete one study unit at a time. If you spend about 7 hours per study unit, you will invest about 91 hours in Part 1 and 70 hours in Part 2. Add 4 hours (broken up because you will refer to each study unit as you need it) to study Study Units 1 through 7 in this *How to Pass the CMA Exam: A System for Success* booklet. Add another 10-20 hours per part for taking customized Practice Exams on problem areas as a cumulative review.

Different people will be able to study for different amounts of time per week. Your completion rate will depend on your personal circumstances (e.g., how familiar you are with the material, your level of education, elapsed time since your degree was earned, how much time you have available to study, how long you can concentrate in one sitting, etc.). Gleim has developed a Study Planner, which is available through Gleim Online, to allow you to personalize your study schedule based on your commitments, limitations, etc. Speak to a Gleim Personal Counselor for assistance in staying on track. Call (888) 874-5346, ext. 498, or email PersonalCounselor@gleim.com.

6.3   WHEN AND WHERE TO STUDY

You should study when you study best, i.e., whenever you are most productive and able to focus. Unfortunately, other activities compete for your time. CMA preparation should not be your lowest priority.

Determine what time-consuming activities you can temporarily give up or defer. Set up a regular schedule with goals regarding how much you will complete in one sitting. This will give you a feeling of accomplishment.

Study wherever you can concentrate. The Gleim **CMA Review System** is presented in multimedia for your convenience. Home, work, public transportation, hotels, libraries, and restaurants are all possible study areas. Find study areas that are quiet, well lit, and free of distractions.

6.4   PRELIMINARY TESTING: GLEIM CMA DIAGNOSTIC QUIZ

The Gleim CMA Diagnostic Quiz provides a representative sample of 40 multiple-choice questions for each exam part. You should use this tool to determine which part of the exam you want to take first and/or how much time you need to devote to studying particular topic areas (i.e., what your strengths and weaknesses are).

When you have completed the quiz, you will be able to access a Review Session, where you can study answer explanations for the correct and incorrect answer choices of the questions you answered incorrectly. You will also have the option to consult with a Personal Counselor in order to better focus your review on any areas in which you have less confidence.

Candidates who have already purchased the Gleim CMA Review System should skip the Diagnostic Quiz and immediately follow the steps on the next page, which incorporate study-unit-specific diagnostic testing.

6.5 HOW TO USE THE GLEIM REVIEW SYSTEM

To ensure that you are using your time effectively, we have formulated a three-step process to apply to each study unit that includes all components (book, CMA Test Prep, Audio Reviews, Gleim Online, and Essay Wizard) together.

Step 1: Diagnostic

a.   Multiple-Choice Quiz #1 (30 minutes, plus 10 minutes for review) – In Gleim Online, complete Multiple-Choice Quiz #1 in 30 minutes. This is a diagnostic quiz, so it is expected that your scores will be lower.

   1)   Immediately following the quiz, review the questions you marked and/or answered incorrectly. This step is essential to identifying your weak areas. Study Unit 4, Subunit 7, has tips on how to learn from your mistakes.

Step 2: Comprehension

a.   Audiovisual Presentation (30 minutes) – This presentation provides an overview of the study unit. The Gleim CMA Audio Review can be substituted for audiovisual presentations.

b.   True/False Quiz (45 minutes) – Complete the True/False quiz in Gleim Online and receive immediate feedback.

c.   Knowledge Transfer Outline (60-90 minutes) – Study the Knowledge Transfer Outline, particularly the troublesome areas identified from your Multiple-Choice Quiz #1 in Step 1. The Knowledge Transfer Outlines can be studied either online or in the books.

d.   Multiple-Choice Quiz #2 (30 minutes, plus 10 minutes for review) – Complete Multiple-Choice Quiz #2 in Gleim Online.

   1)   Immediately following the quiz, review the questions you marked and/or answered incorrectly. This step is an essential learning activity. Study Unit 4, Subunit 7, has tips on how to learn from your mistakes.

Step 3: Application

a.   CMA Test Prep (60 minutes, plus 20 minutes for review) – Complete two 20-question quizzes in CMA Test Prep using the Practice Exam feature. Spend 30 minutes taking each quiz and then spend about 10 minutes reviewing each quiz as needed.

b.   Essay Scenario (30 minutes, plus 10 minutes for review) – Complete the essay scenario in Gleim Online. Budget 30 minutes to complete the scenario and spend about 10 minutes reviewing.

Additional Assistance

1.   Gleim Instruct Supplemental Videos (watch as needed) – These videos discuss multiple-choice questions and essay scenarios that test the topics candidates find the most difficult.

2.   Gleim Essay Wizard – For additional practice answering essays, complete scenarios as needed.

Final Review

1.   CMA Exam Rehearsal (4 hours/240 minutes) – Take the Exam Rehearsal at the beginning of your final review stage. It contains 100 multiple-choice questions and 2 essay scenarios, just like the CMA exams. This will help you identify where you should focus during the remainder of your final review.

2.   CMA Test Prep (10-20 hours) – Use Test Prep to focus on your weak areas identified from your Exam Rehearsal. Also, be sure to do a cumulative review to refresh yourself with topics you learned at the beginning of your studies. View your performance chart to make sure you are scoring 75% or higher.

The times mentioned above are recommendations based on prior candidate feedback and how long you have to answer questions on the actual exam. Each candidate's time spent in any area will vary depending on proficiency and familiarity with the subject matter.

> **The following is a detailed description of Gleim products that will prepare you to pass the CMA exam according to the steps given on the previous page.**

6.6 CMA GLEIM ONLINE

CMA Gleim Online is a multi-platform self-study review program delivered via the Internet. It is divided into two courses (one for each part of the CMA exam) and contains ICMA-released multiple-choice and essay questions in an interface designed to emulate the CMA exam.

Each course contains

- Gleim Instruct supplemental videos
- Audiovisual presentations
- Comprehensive review book outlines
- Hundreds of multiple-choice and true/false questions
- Ample essay question practice
- Core concepts with overview of each study unit's key points

CMA Gleim Online provides you with access to a Personal Counselor, a real person who will provide support to ensure your competitive edge. CMA Gleim Online is a great way to get confidence as you prepare with Gleim. This confidence will continue during and after the exam.

6.7 GLEIM ESSAY WIZARD

The Gleim Essay Wizard is a training program that focuses on the essay questions appearing on both parts of the CMA exam. These online courses provide at least two essays per study unit, as well as test-taking tips from Dr. Gleim to help you be in control.

6.8 GLEIM OUTLINES

The Gleim CMA outlines can be accessed via CMA Gleim Online or the Review books. The CMA Review books are the perfect component for the times you do not have access to the Internet. The outlines have the following features to make studying easier:

1. **Examples:** Extended, illustrative examples, both hypothetical and those drawn from actual events, are set off in shaded, bordered boxes.

EXAMPLE

A company issued 50,000 shares of its $1 par-value common stock. The market price of the stock was $17 per share on the day of issue.

Cash (50,000 shares × $17 market price)	$850,000	
Common stock (50,000 shares × $1 par value)		$ 50,000
Additional paid-in capital -- common (difference)		800,000

The balances of cash, common stock, and additional paid-in capital were increased by $850,000, $50,000, and $800,000, respectively.

---

2. **Gleim Success Tips:** These tips supplement the core exam material by suggesting how certain topics might be presented on the exam or how you should prepare for an issue.

 Management accountants are expected to know the theory and how to complete detailed calculations for the topics covered in this study unit. To provide a more focused approach to studying, Gleim has broken up the theoretical questions and computational questions of the different cost allocation techniques into separate subunits. CMA candidates should expect a mix of both theory and computational questions on the CMA exam.

3. **International Standards Differences:** When international standards differ significantly from U.S. GAAP, we note the differences. Currently, this feature applies to the Financial Reporting section of Part 1 only.

IFRS Difference

No items are classified as extraordinary, either on the statement of comprehensive income or in the notes.

6.9 CMA TEST PREP

CMA Test Prep is an online question bank that offers unlimited Practice Exams to give you unprecedented studying potential. Twenty-question Practice Exams in CMA Test Prep will help you to focus on your weaker areas. Make it a game: How much can you improve?

Our CMA Test Prep Practice Exams force you to commit to your answer choice before looking at answer explanations; thus, you are preparing under true exam conditions. They also keep track of your time and performance history for each study unit, which is available in either a table or graphical format. Your performance data can be accessed on any computer or mobile device so you can study anywhere.

6.10 GLEIM AUDIO REVIEW

Gleim CMA Audio Reviews provide an average of 30 minutes of quality review for each study unit. Each review provides an overview of the outline for each study unit in the CMA Review books. The purpose is to get candidates "started" so they can relate to the questions they will answer before reading the study outlines in each study unit.

The audios get to the point, as does the entire Gleim System for Success. We are working to get you through the CMA exam with minimum time, cost, and frustration. You can listen to two short sample audio reviews on our website at www.gleim.com/DemosCMA.

6.11 IF YOU HAVE QUESTIONS ABOUT GLEIM MATERIALS

Content-specific questions about our materials will be answered most rapidly if they are sent to us via the easily accessible feedback forms within the online study components. Our team of accounting experts will give your correspondence thorough consideration and a prompt response.

There are two methods for submitting an inquiry to our accounting experts:

1. The preferred method is to utilize the "Submit Question Feedback" link that appears beneath the answer explanations of all questions in a Review Session. Use this method if you have an inquiry about a question in Gleim Online, Test Prep, Exam Rehearsals, Diagnostic Quizzes, or Essay Wizard.

2. For inquiries regarding your Gleim Review book or Test Prep Software Download, please visit www.gleim.com/questions and submit your inquiry using the on-screen form.

In order for us to deliver your response directly to your Personal Classroom, you will need to log in to your Gleim account to submit your inquiry.

Questions regarding the information in this Introduction (study suggestions, studying plans, exam specifics) should be emailed to PersonalCounselor@gleim.com.

Questions concerning orders, prices, shipments, or payments should be sent via email to customerservice@gleim.com and will be promptly handled by our competent and courteous customer service staff.

For technical support, you may use our automated technical support service at www.gleim.com/support, email us at support@gleim.com, or call us at (888) 874-5346.

STUDY UNIT SEVEN
HOW TO TAKE THE CMA EXAM

(5 pages of outline)

The purpose of this study unit is to focus on what to expect on exam day and how to react. It includes a general explanation of examination site instructions, rules, and procedures. You have to know what to expect so you are not distracted from your mission of **passing the exam**!

7.1 A POSITIVE MENTAL ATTITUDE

You are in control with Gleim CMA Review, which is based upon a systematic, thorough review of all material tested on the CMA exam. The Gleim method does not involve guessing about what will appear on the next CMA exam. **You will be prepared for any and all questions.** If a question appears difficult to you, it will be **more** difficult for other candidates.

You have done your best to prepare, and you will do your best when you take the exam. No one can ask for more. Be proud.

7.2 EXAM SITE LOCATION

Prometric exam sites vary in how they are operated. Talk to someone who took an exam at the site you plan to use. Ask him or her for information about the site and for any suggestions (s)he might have. Additionally, make sure you know where the exam site is and how to get there.

A few days prior to taking your exam, call your Prometric Testing Center and confirm your appointment; leave as little as possible to chance.

7.3 THE DAY OF YOUR CMA EXAM

On the day of your exam, plan on getting to the testing site about 30-60 minutes ahead of your appointment time. Leave all study materials in your car or at home, but don't forget your calculator. If you must, you can bring snacks, drinks, etc., to the testing site, but you must leave these items in a locker or a designated area.

Be sure to wear comfortable clothes. Sweats, shorts, and jeans are very appropriate. Wear layers according to your usual body temperature because you will not be allowed to remove any outerwear once you are in the testing room. Generally, wear what you wear when you are most comfortable studying. Remember that coats, umbrellas, books, and attaché cases cannot be accommodated at the exam site. Thus, you should not take something that you do not want to lose.

7.4 PROMETRIC TEST CENTER RULES

Prometric will NOT allow you to bring anything except an approved calculator (see below) into the exam room. Do **not** bring any study notes or materials to the exam on your person, e.g., in pockets. If any such notes fall out of your pocket during the exam, you will be accused of cheating. Additional rules and procedures are outlined below and on the next page.

1. You must arrive at the test center at least 30 minutes before your scheduled appointment. If you arrive after your scheduled appointment time, you may forfeit your appointment and not be eligible to have your examination fees refunded. When you arrive, turn off all cell phones and other electronic devices.

2. You will be required to sign the Prometric Log Book when you enter the center.

3. You must place any personal belongings, including any outerwear, etc., that you remove during the exam, in the storage lockers provided by the test center.

4. You are required to present either a valid passport or two other original forms of non-expired identification, one with a photograph, both with your signature. Approved photo IDs are a driver's license, military ID, national country ID card, credit card with photo, bank debit card with signature, or company ID. Student IDs and Social Security cards are not acceptable. If you leave the testing room for any reason, you will be required to show your identification to be readmitted. You **will not be** permitted into the examination without proper identification.

5. For exams taken on or after September 1, 2013, your fingerprint(s) will be captured.

6. You will be escorted to a workstation by test center staff. You must remain in your seat during the examination, except when authorized to get up and leave the testing room by test center staff. You may take breaks if you wish, but remember: The clock will not stop while you are away!

7. You may choose what kind of calculator you would like to bring from six specific options. See the next page for a more complete description of allowable calculators.

8. When you finish the examination, quietly leave the testing room, turn in your scratch paper, and sign the test center log book. The test center staff will dismiss you after completing all necessary procedures.

For more information on Prometric regulations, accommodations, testing experience, etc., visit www.prometric.com/en-us/for-test-takers/Prepare-for-Test-Day/frequently-asked-questions/ or see the ICMA's Candidate Handbook.

7.5 CMA CANDIDATE MISCONDUCT AND CHEATING

The CMA Candidate Handbook states the ICMA's policy on cheating as follows:

"Cheating will not be tolerated, and all instances of suspected cheating will be fully investigated. Examinees who are caught cheating will have their grades invalidated and will be disqualified from future examinations. Cheating includes, but is not limited to, the following; copying answers from another candidate during the exam, using unauthorized materials during the exam, helping another candidate during the exam, removing exam materials from the testing room, divulging exam questions, and/or falsifying credentials. For those already certified by the ICMA, failure to comply with the non-disclosure policy or the subsequent discovery of cheating will be considered a violation of the IMA Statement of Ethical Professional Practice and could result in revocation of the certificate."

7.6 CALCULATORS

Simple six-function calculators are permitted (i.e., addition, subtraction, multiplication, division, square root, percent). Alternatively, candidates may choose to bring a Texas Instruments BAII Plus, Hewlett Packard 10bII, HP 12C, or HP 12C Platinum calculator. Feedback from candidates who have already taken at least one part of the exam using only the six-function calculator, however, has shown that the simpler calculator will suffice for the CMA. Candidates should rest assured that time value tables are available for use on questions that demand them.

Candidates are responsible for providing their own calculators. You should be thoroughly experienced in the operations of your calculator; we suggest that you study with it prior to taking the exam. Make sure it has fresh batteries just prior to the examination.

- Consider bringing a backup calculator with you.
- The calculator must be small, quiet, and battery- or solar-powered so it will not be distracting to other candidates.
- The calculator must not use any type of tape.
- The calculator must be nonprogrammable.

7.7 BEGINNING YOUR EXAM

After you check in with your ID, you will be escorted to a computer station. There will be candidates taking many different exams in the room with you (financial exams, medical exams, etc.)

Prometric will provide you with an opportunity to view an abbreviated exam introduction. Work through it so you do not miss anything. As you begin the exam, you will do fine because you have experienced the Gleim Prometric look-alike screens.

7.8 COMPUTER PROBLEMS AT THE EXAM SITE

There is about a 1-in-100 chance that you will encounter a computer problem at the exam site. The most common problem requires staff to reboot your computer. At most, you will lose a minute of testing time, according to Prometric. If you have a computer problem, stop and tell/show the exam proctor. Do NOT erase any messages on the screen. Do NOT attempt to circumvent or fix the system. It is a Prometric problem. Note the time it occurred and when it is rectified for your appropriate use in the future.

Please report all computer problems in detail to Gleim by emailing CMA@gleim.com.

Minimize your risk of computer problems by practicing your use of the Prometric look-alike computer screens in CMA Gleim Online.

Gleim Pass the CMA Video Series

You can bring a calculator to the CMA exam. But which one should you choose? How do you avoid any calculator crises during the exam? The Gleim "Pass the CMA Exam" video series provides answers to these questions and much more!

www.gleim.com/CMAVideos

7.9 TIME MANAGEMENT

A major issue on the CMA exam is time management. The only help you get is hours, minutes, and seconds remaining in your test with no guidance for breaks or time allocation within each section.

We have prepared a Gleim Time Management System that will work for both parts of the exam. You have to budget 3 hours for 100 multiple-choice questions and at least 1 hour (more if you finished your multiple-choice early) for two essay scenarios with multiple questions each. Recall that you cannot go back to the multiple-choice section once you have moved on to essays.

The key to success is to become proficient in (1) answering multiple-choice questions at a rate of 1.5 minutes per question and (2) answering an essay scenario in half of your time remaining regardless of how many questions it contains.

1. Here is our suggestion for successfully managing your time on the CMA exam:

    Multiple-choice section: 100 questions @ 1.5 minutes per question   150 min.
                                                 Review of unanswered, marked questions   15 min.
                                                 Section complete in 165 minutes, leaving 15 minutes
                                                 to carry over to essay section

    Essay section: 60 min. standard time allocation + 15 min.   75 min.
                                         1 scenario with 1 question   37 min.
                                         1 scenario with 3 questions   37 min.
                                         (Per question   12 min.)
                                         Section complete in about 75 minutes

2. Since the computer screen shows hours:minutes:seconds remaining, you need to focus on the hour:minutes, NOT time on your watch or minutes. Throughout your practice exam questions, always think in terms of hours:minutes. Thus, on a perfect exam using the times above, you would start each section with the following hours:minutes displayed on-screen:

    Multiple-choice section: 3 hours   0 minutes
    Essay section: 1 hour   15 minutes

3. Next, develop shorthand for hours:minutes. Signify 3 hours, 0 minutes as 03:00 and 1 hour, 15 minutes as 01:15. Thus, the start times for the two sections will be

    Multiple-choice section: 03:00
    Essay section: 01:15

4. Use one page of scratch paper (provided at Prometric) for your Gleim Time Management System at the exam (see our examples on the next page).

    a. For the multiple-choice section, as soon as the exam starts, write 1, 21, 41, 61, etc., in the left column followed by 03:00, 02:30, 02:00, 01:30, etc., respectively. As you complete each set of 20 questions, note when you finish, and then start the next set.

Multiple-Choice Question Time Management

QuestionSet	Start	Finish	Notes
1	03:00		
21	02:30		
41	02:00		
61	01:30		

b.   Then, move on to your essay section and create your time management sheet for essays. Enter your starting time remaining (which will be at least 60 minutes), the number of questions in each scenario, how much time you have to answer all the questions in each scenario, and when you finish.

Essay Time Management

Scenario	Questions	Time	Start	Finish	Comments
1	1	30	60		
2	2 3 4	30			

Note that the image above is an example only. The number of questions per scenario will vary, as well as how much total time you have to spend (based on when you completed your multiple-choice section). It is important to use a sheet of scratch paper to help you manage your time at the exam.

5.   It is essential to use CMA Test Prep and Gleim Online to practice answering multiple-choice questions under exam conditions. The expectation is 1.5 minutes per question and a 15-minute review of unanswered/marked questions. This requires you to become proficient at your multiple-choice question-answering technique (see Study Unit 4, Subunit 5).

6.   You must also practice essays under exam conditions. Use Gleim Online and Essay Wizard to practice allocating the correct amount of time per question in each scenario. Gleim Online provides one essay scenario per study unit, and Essay Wizard provides at least two additional essays to practice on. All essays in the Gleim system are based on topics tested according to the ICMA CSOs.

CMA EXAM WORKSHEET

PART _____

	DATE COMPLETED	DATE RECEIVED

1. Apply for membership to the IMA **and** enter the ICMA's Certification Program. ☐

   a. Receive your IMA member number. ☐

2. Register for the exam part(s) and window of your choosing within 12 months, and pay the indicated fees. ☐

   a. Receive the CMA Exam Authorization Letter via email (provides your authorization number and testing window confirmation). ☐

3. Register at Prometric.com with your IMA authorization number and email address. ☐

4. Schedule your exam at Prometric. ☐

   a. Receive confirmation email. When you receive it, print it out and paper-clip it to this worksheet to take to the exam site on exam day. ☐

5. Go to www.gleim.com/feedbackCMA as soon as you have completed your exam to let us know how well Gleim prepared you! ☐

Exam Date _____   Exam Time _____

Exam Location _____   *[Print out directions to site and paper-clip them to this worksheet.]*

Checklist of Items to Bring

IMA member and authorization numbers _____

Appointment confirmation _____

Valid/current identification _____

Directions to testing center _____

Approved calculator (optional) _____

GLEIM® - Experts in Accounting Education

GLEIM CPA REVIEW SYSTEM

Includes: Gleim Online, Gleim Instruct, Review Books, CPA Test Prep, Simulation Wizard, Audio Review, Exam Rehearsal™, *How to Pass the CPA Exam: A System for Success* booklet, plus bonus Book Bag.

$989.95 x _____ = $_____

Also available by exam section (does not include Book Bag).

GLEIM CMA REVIEW SYSTEM

Includes: Gleim Online, Gleim Instruct, Review Books, CMA Test Prep, Essay Wizard, Audio Review, Exam Rehearsal™, *How to Pass the CMA Exam: A System for Success* booklet, plus bonus Book Bag.

$899.95 x _____ = $_____

Also available by exam part (does not include Book Bag).

GLEIM CIA REVIEW SYSTEM (New 3-Part Exam)

Includes: Gleim Online, Review Books, CIA Test Prep, Audio Review, Exam Rehearsal™, *How to Pass the CIA Exam: A System for Success* booklet, plus bonus Book Bag.

$724.95 x _____ = $_____

Also available by exam part (does not include Book Bag).

GLEIM EA REVIEW SYSTEM

Includes: Gleim Online, Review Books, EA Test Prep, Audio Review, Exam Rehearsal™, *How to Pass the EA Exam: A System for Success* booklet, plus bonus Book Bag.

$629.95 x _____ = $_____

Also available by exam part (does not include Book Bag).

GLEIM ANNUAL FILING SEASON PROGRAM

Includes: 6-hour Annual Federal Tax Refresher (AFTR) Course, all other required CE courses.

$69.95 x _____ = $_____

Meets all IRS Annual Filing Season Program requirements.

"THE GLEIM EQE SERIES" EXAM QUESTIONS AND EXPLANATIONS

Includes: 5 Books and EQE Test Prep.

$124.95 x _____ = $_____

Also available by part.

GLEIM ONLINE CPE

Try a FREE 4-hour course at gleim.com/cpe
- Easy-to-Complete
- Informative
- Effective

Contact
GLEIM® PUBLICATIONS
for further assistance:

gleim.com
888.874.5346
sales@gleim.com

SUBTOTAL $_____

Complete your order on the next page

Subject to change without notice.

GLEIM® PUBLICATIONS, INC.

P. O. Box 12848   Gainesville, FL 32604

TOLL FREE:	888.874.5346
LOCAL:	352.375.0772
FAX:	352.375.6940
INTERNET:	gleim.com
EMAIL:	sales@gleim.com

Customer service is available (Eastern Time):
8:00 a.m. - 7:00 p.m., Mon. - Fri.
9:00 a.m. - 2:00 p.m., Saturday
Please have your credit card ready,
or save time by ordering online!

SUBTOTAL (from previous page) $_____
Add applicable sales tax for shipments within Florida. _____
Shipping (nonrefundable) 15.95

TOTAL $_____

Email us for prices/instructions on shipments outside the 48 contiguous states, or simply order online.

NAME (please print) _____

ADDRESS _____ Apt. _____
(street address required for UPS/Federal Express)

CITY _____ STATE_____ ZIP_____

____ MC/VISA/DISC/AMEX ____ Check/M.O. Daytime Telephone (____)_____

Credit Card No. _____ - _____ - _____ - _____

Exp. _____/_____ Signature _____
   Month / Year

Email address _____

1. We process and ship orders daily, within one business day over 98.8% of the time. Call by 3:00 pm for same day service.

2. Gleim Publications, Inc. guarantees the immediate refund of all resalable texts, unopened and un-downloaded Test Prep Software, and unopened and un-downloaded audios returned within 30 days of purchase. Accounting and Academic online Test Prep and other online courses may be canceled within 30 days of purchase if no more than the first study unit or lesson has been accessed. In addition, Online CPE courses may be canceled within 30 days of adding the course to your Personal Transcript if the Outline has not yet been accessed. Accounting Exam Rehearsals and Practice Exams may be canceled within 30 days of purchase if they have not been started. Aviation Test Prep Online may be canceled within 30 days of purchase if no more than the first study unit has been accessed. Other Aviation online courses may be canceled within 30 days of purchase if no more than two study units have been accessed. This policy applies only to products that are purchased directly from Gleim Publications, Inc. No refunds will be provided on opened or downloaded Test Prep Software or audios, partial returns of package sets, or shipping and handling charges. Any freight charges incurred for returned or refused packages will be the purchaser's responsibility. For more information regarding the Gleim Return Policy, please contact our offices at (888) 874-5346.

3. Please PHOTOCOPY this order form for others.

4. No CODs. Orders from individuals must be prepaid

Subject to change without notice. 08/14

For updates and other important information, visit our website.

GLEIM
KNOWLEDGE
TRANSFER
SYSTEMS®

gleim.com